If you make the move, God will make the way.

I0159783

COURAGEOUS
FAITH

A REMARKABLE STORY OF FAITH
AND MIRACULOUS HEALING

VICTORY LIFE
MEDIA

JERRY BONSU

Published in France by VICTORY LIFE MEDIA an imprint of JBM

JERRY BONSU MINISTRIES
http://www.jerrybonsu.org

VLM books may be ordered through booksellers or by visiting **www.jerrybonsu.org**. VLM Speakers Bureau provides a wide range of authors for speaking events. To find out more, email us: **victorylifemedia@gmail.com**.

French National Library-in-Publication Data
Dépôt légal: 05/2018

Book cover art by Victory Life Media Team

Printed in the United States of America

ISBN: 978-2-9541960-6-0

For further information or permission, contact us on the Internet:

VICTORY LIFE MEDIA "Empowering our Generation for the next Generation" **www.victorylifemedia.com**.

CONTENTS

INTRODUCTION

The Woman With An Issue Of Blood

Have you ever been desperate for help in your life? What do you do when you have a problem, and every possible solution you try fails you? You have tried all you can do with your own strength but nothing works; you even try to get friends and family to help you with your problem, but nobody can help you through your trials and affliction.

When in such a situation, it can be very easy to give up hoping that things will get better. It can also be very easy for one to give up on life. However, the Bible talks of a woman who had a disease and who was desperate for help after having tried all that she could on her own and still failed. (see Mark 5:21-34)

The story of this woman takes place within a larger story. Jesus is on His way to Jairus (*a synagogue leader*) house to heal his dying daughter when an unnamed woman causes an interruption to His progress. What we know about the woman is, first, she had a bleeding condition, and the issue had continued for *twelve* years.

Second, she had spent all her money on treatments from many doctors, and nothing had helped; in fact, the blood issue had only grown worse. She went to the best doctors of her time, but they gave her no help and no hope. She may have even suffered from her treatment as much as she suffered from her problem.

Year after year went on without any chance in the natural for this woman. But one day, she heard that Jesus was coming to her town. News had spread of the miracles that were taking place everywhere He went. I can imagine something deep on the inside of this woman rose up and said, *"This is your season. This is your time to get well."* When Jesus arrived, of course a large crowd gathered. When the woman saw all the people around Him she may have thought, *"I'll never get His attention. It's so crowded and I'm weak. I just don't think I can do this."* She could have almost missed her season.

I can imagine that she was fighting those negative thoughts just like we all would if we were in her position. I can also imagine her encouraging herself and saying over and over, *"If I can just get close enough to touch His garment, I know that I will be whole."* The Scripture tells us that she kept pressing her way through the crowd until she was just close enough to Jesus to reach out and touch the edge of His robe.

According to the Jewish Law she was declared to be ceremonially unclean due to her bleeding issue (see Leviticus 15:25-27). This meant that she would not have been permitted to enter the temple for Jewish religious ceremonies… Anything or anyone she touched became unclean as well. The fact that she was in the crowd pressing around Jesus means that each person who bumped into her would have become unclean too — including Jesus. But, after twelve years of suffering, she was obviously desperate for a miracle.

The Bible says, as soon as she touches Jesus, her bleeding stops and she knows she has been healed. In an instant, Jesus does what no doctor in twelve years had been able to. This proves the amazing healing power of Christ! (see Mark 5:27-29)

What is interesting is that Jesus actually felt her touch of faith. If you think about it, He was in a huge crowd of people. They were bumping into Him and touching Him left and right. But this woman's contact wasn't just an ordinary touch. It was a touch of faith and expectancy; and it impacted Jesus. This woman released her faith fully expecting to be healed, and Jesus felt the healing virtue (power) flow out of Him. Instantly, she was made whole! (see Mark 5:27-29). I love that we are told it was instantly… how good our God is to share these details with us!

She was made well by her faith in Jesus. She finally believed that only Jesus would help her. Her faith in her finances failed; her faith in the doctors failed… but her faith in Jesus did not fail! I believe that this woman's faith is something we could all take a lesson from. Oh yes! She wasn't just a woman with an issue of blood… That is how the text describes her. But when we read between the lines and fit *together* all the puzzle pieces, we also see that she was a woman of strong faith.

Beloved, it's our faith that opens the door for God's power to work in our lives. I wrote this book to encourage you to live beyond the normal limits of life and experience the unlimited power of God on a regular basis. Through this life-changing book, I want to challenge you to overcome your barriers, conquer your fear, realize your goals, and start over when you fail!

No matter how many defilements you bear. No matter how many disappointments you have faced. No matter how many times your hopes have been dashed. No matter how many people have rejected you as though you are less than. Like the woman with the issue of blood... Are you willing to go the extreme to be with Jesus? To receive the miracles you so desperately need from God? Ready to work your faith, hoping against all odds, and keep pressing in to Jesus for your breakthrough? If the answer is yes, then keep on reading!

My prayer is that as you read through this book, God helps you to reach out to Him and claim His power in the Mighty name of Jesus! May He increase your faith so that you can receive all the blessings He has in store for you.

Today, dare to believe that God can change everything. Dare to believe the unbelievable and receive the unimaginable. Your miracle is on the way. Your hope is always safe in Jesus!

If you make the move, God will make the way.

COURAGEOUS
FAITH

CHAPTER ONE

NO MOVEMENT!
NO MIRACLE!

DO YOU KNOW THAT EVERY INSTANCE of faith in the Bible required action? No miracle or otherwise will come into your life without action on your part. As the matter of fact, miracles don't just happen by chance. When you ask the Lord for a miracle, He will usually give you something to do. This is your part to play in the miracle — an opportunity to put your faith into action.

I have found that God is moved to action by our faith, even when He is in the *middle* of doing something else! The story of the woman in Mark 5 demonstrates to us the place of faith in action. She took a step of faith (action). She pressed through a crowd towards Jesus declaring her faith. She knew that she had no choice but to come to Jesus. She came trembling. She took a huge risk and managed to tell Him the whole story of her miserable life, her feeling of despair and the burden of being an outcast.

In verse 27, the Bible tells us that she believed all she needed to do was to touch JESUS and she would be healed. As He passes her, from behind, she just reaches out and touches the fringe of His robe... and the Bible says, "Immediately the bleeding stopped and she could feel that she had been healed."

Jesus did not speak any words. She was not given instructions to follow in order to receive healing. That act of faith—just to reach out and touch His garment was enough to bring her complete healing. Because of Jesus response to her, we know that her act of faith brought the healing.

Jesus said to her,

*"Daughter, your **faith** has healed you.*
Go in peace and be free from your sickness."

Mark 5:34 (NLV)

Beloved, if you want to have access to your own miracle, you need to initiate it through faith. As Bishop David Oyedepo said, "Faith is an act; and it is that act that compels the release of virtue (power), which we later celebrate as testimonies." Acting what you believe and confess is what turns on the virtue for *performance*. Every release of divine virtue is traceable to a definite act. Without an act, there can be no release of virtue!

Your act is the connection that your faith requires to perform. Faith without an act is like a body without life! Do you know that you will never live a healthy life until you start acting healthy? It takes healthy acts to become a healthy saint. You cannot keep looking like an unhealthy person and expect to be healed.

God is busy weighing your actions to determine His interventions in your life. If your actions are found wanting... you may die in want, because you have blocked the access to God's intervention. Friend, action is the only way to prove that you believe. If you do not act out to what you claim to believe, then you don't believe it.

The woman with the issue of blood got her miracle because after she had heard so much about Jesus, she moved by faith, she said in her heart, *"If I should only touch his garment I shall be healed."* And as we read, she did not stop there. She went further by making her way through the crowd, to touch the hem of Jesus garment, and the switch for the miraculous was turned loose! Virtue, the omnipotent power of faith, began to flow, and her shame ended instantly!

Understand this, faith does not leave you with only what to recite or confess, but also with what to do. Faith is not just cheap talk, faith is great acts! It is more than thinking, talking, or having convictions about Jesus. Faith is action! It is movement; it is activity. Faith is something you do. "If people say they have faith, but do nothing, their faith is worth nothing" (see James 2:14, NCV)

Before I share with you in the next chapter about how to release the power of faith, I want you to know this; Big things take big faith... and big faith takes effort. Live at the level that your miracle requires! What does that mean? If you need a miracle then you will have to live at a level in God that will support a miracle. I get prayer requests all the time. They all go something like this, "*Please man of God, pray for me, I have a terrible issue and I desperately need God's help.*" Yes, I can pray for them, and I do, but real help comes when people rise up themselves and do the things they need to do. Remember, faith without works is dead!

The woman refused to lay there and die! She refused to let her circumstance determine her faith! Her fear of failure did not keep her back. Fear of not being worthy did not stop her. She had a need and she knew Jesus was the answer to it. She reached out and accepted what He offers to all of us—healing and becoming whole in Him. (see Colossians 2:9-14)

It is not only your words that matter to heaven, your action is equally important. "…for the Lord is a God of knowledge, and by him actions are weighed." (see 1 Samuel 2:3) I titled this chapter "*No Movement!… No Miracle!*" because I firmly believe that every miracle must be preceded through an action of faith. Be like this woman who did not give up hope. Push through the crowd of your own doubts, fears, and pain. Reach out your hand in faith to Jesus… Get His mind. Soak in His presence. Stay your ground until the miracle flows downstream to you.

Always remember, regardless of the scope of your problem, God is ready, willing and able to relive that burden from you and provide for you what you need. Step into your miracle now! Don't look at the crowd… focus on Jesus! If you make the move… God will make the way!

If you make the move, God will make the way.

COURAGEOUS
FAITH

VICTORY LIFE
M E D I A

CHAPTER TWO

FAITH
MANIFESTED IN COURAGE

EVERY STEP OF FAITH REQUIRES courage. When you study the lives of the people God used in the Bible, there is an obvious connection between faith and courage. If our faith is strong, we will be strong and courageous. But if our faith is weak, we will lack the courage we need to stand strong as God's children.

To believe in the Kingdom of God in a world that rejects God requires faith. Just like Abraham (the father of faith), you must be fully convinced that God is able to do what He has promised, and you must act accordingly. Then your faith will be reckoned to you as righteousness. (see Romans 4:21–22)

In this chapter, I would like to share with you about courageous faith; the kind of faith that allows us to experience stability in the middle of instability. The kind of faith, which believes that what God is about to do, eyes has not seen, ear has not heard, and no mind has imagined. (see 1 Corinthians 2:9) But first, let us see what Faith is.

According to the Scripture, "...*faith is the substance of*

things hoped for, the evidence of things not seen." (see Hebrews 11:1)

Faith is belief with strong conviction; firm belief in something for which there may be no tangible proof; complete trust in or devotion to. Faith is reaching out into the unknown and grasping onto it. Faith believes without seeing. Faith trusts when there is no reason to trust. That belief in faith is the core of who you are.

Faith is defines as a spiritual substance, which connects man with God for divine intervention. According to Hebrews 11:6, you cannot connect with God except through faith. Faith is not a feeling; it is a concrete, tangible force by which people obtain good report. It is a spiritual force that connects the natural with the Supernatural. Faith can do a lot of things in your life if you let it. It will grow you and allow you to do things you never thought yourself capable of. It will turn you into a dreamer who really believes that with God, all things are possible (see Matthew 19:26).

As I said earlier, faith is very vital to our walk as Christians. Faith is an expression of our confidence in God and His Word. Faith in God gives you strength. And it also gives you courage. When I say strength, I don't mean a physical strength to fight bullies. I mean the inner resolve to withstand turmoil.

Faith is a winning weapon in the battles of life. It is what silences the devil. (see Ephesians 6:16) Without it you cannot walk in victory! Faith is a weapon of destruction against the enemy. Faith doesn't overcome some of satan's attacks. It overcomes ALL of them. In fact, faith is the mightiest of all weapons. When our spirits are armed with faith, we may go confidently into any battle. We may have expectation of winning. We may know before we fight that victory is ours. We may face our adversary with calm confidence and with a consciousness of an indwelling power that is greater than his power.

Having a faith as small as a muster seed is all that is required to make things happen. Where our faith stops is where our testimony stops; Faith is our life wire! Nothing works without it.

- **We live by faith** (see Habakkuk 2:4, Romans 1:17, Hebrews 10:38).

- **We also walk by faith** (see 2 Corinthians 5:7).

- **We overcome by faith** (see 1 John 5:4).

- **We can only stand by faith** (see 2 Corinthians 1:24).

- **We are kept by faith** (1 Peter 1:5).

Healing also comes by faith. As the matter of fact, faith is our guarantee for divine health and healing, as Jesus would so often say to the sick that came to Him, *"Be it to you according to thy faith."* Faith is a major key that opens the door to miracles. If you study the Bible and history, you find that every time God moves on earth and does a miracle, it's because somebody believed. Jesus says, *"Have faith in God! If you have faith in God and don't doubt, you can tell this mountain to get up and jump into the sea, and it will. Everything you ask for in prayer will be yours, if you only have faith."* (see Mark 11:22-24, CEV)

We must have faith in God. He is our Leader. The army that does not have confidence in the ability and courage of its leader is half defeated before it goes into battle.

The Courageous Faith

When you think about courageous faith, what comes to mind? Courage has largely moved from real life to the realm of stories. Look at literature and movies, and you can quickly build an impressive list of the courageous. Look at society, and you will find it a much more difficult task. Many people think courage have to do with warfare and bloodshed and the crash of armies on the battlefield.

When many of us think of courage we usually think of death-defying acts or great heroic sacrifices; a fireman rushing into a burning building to save *trapped* children (family)... a policeman putting himself in harm's way to protect innocent people... a soldier dashing across a mine field to rescue *trapped* comrades. We think of the astronauts on Apollo 13, the survivors of the Holocaust or some of the famous Human Rights activists.

I don't deny or doubt in the least that those things are part of what courage is all about; however, if that is all that courage means, most of us are left out because most of us won't ever literally be on a battlefield.

I have been pondering about the many faces of courage. This is what I think courage is; It is the state or quality of mind or spirit that enables one to face *danger*, fear, or vicissitudes with self-possession, confidence (boldness), and resolution; Bravery! In other words, it is the ability to do what scares us, to act on our beliefs despite threats of danger, to show strength in face of grief or pain.

Mark Twain wrote; "*Courage is resistance to fear, mastery of fear, not absence of fear.*" Courage, according to the Scriptures, is seemingly something that God wants to help each of His children develop. We can see from the Bible how God told Joshua over and over again to "BE STRONG AND COURAGEOUS." (see Joshua 1:9, Deuteronomy 31:6) Jesus often told His followers, "Be of good courage," or, "Do not be afraid." There is an excellent reason for such instructions from our Lord and Savior. People controlled by terror are void of courage. People who have no courage have lost the ability to act by faith.

God is calling us to be bold... To be strong and courageous! If you have the tendency to not take chances in life because you are afraid of making mistakes, God wants you to know He is pleased with you when you try. It doesn't matter if you don't do everything exactly right. What matters is that you step out in faith, believing God will help you!

The woman with the issue of blood had faith and courage. Just think–living twelve years without modern day medicine or medical knowledge on how to help her or every why she was suffering this issue of blood. The fact that she was constantly bleeding must have scared her. Yet, never in the story is it mentioned that she wished to die or gave up trying. She kept going to doctors and when she heard of Jesus, went to Him. This woman kept hope alive those twelve years. And the amazing thing is that, dispite the Mosaic law, she was courageous enough to tell the truth out loud that she had touched Jesus. This is **courageous faith**!

Courageous faith believes that just one touch from God can change everything. Courageous faith is confident that God cannot and will not make a mistake. Courageous faith knows that God cannot be wrong. Courageous faith is confident that God can never be defeated. It is a kind of confidence that can strengthen and sustain us.

One of the biggest lessons that we can learn from this woman is to have courageous faith. Not just faith in Christ as our Savior, but faith in Him as our Healer, our Provider, our Hope, our Redeemer, our Advocate, our Peace, our Joy, our Love, our Hapiness, our Comforter and Counselor in the midst of trouble, our Victory, our Glory, our Protector, our Shepherd, our God and Abba Father... our EVERYTHING!

You see, courage is built, courage is revealed, and courage is power. A courageous person does what God wants him to do, regardless of the consequences. And the good news is that, God loves courageous people! Why? Because it takes courage to obey God. It takes courage to be a true Christian—a follower of Christ!

As we read earlier, there is a direct link between faith and courage. Faith is trust in the promises of God that gives us confidence and courage to act without fear. Courage is always produced by faith... and it is one of the greatest manifestations of it. Daring faith requires taking risk. It requires the courage to step up and face the giants... and to face the unknown. It might be easier to stay in your comfort zone, but when you bravely step out to where God has called you, history is made and lives are changed forever.

One of my favorite preachers, Kathryn Kuhlman once said, *"Faith and courage is something that life requires of each of us."* I know, the world will try to beat down your act of faith, which is why it is so important to develop your confidence in God's faithfulness to you. You can develop this confidence by reading your Bible every day, meditating on what it says, speaking the Word of God out loud, praying, and believing God loves you. Routinely doing this helps establish the Word inside you. It will take root and give you courage and confidence you didn't have before.

"For the word of God is living and powerful, and sharper than any two-edged sword, piercing even to the division of soul and spirit, and of joints and marrow, and is a discerner of the thoughts and intents of the heart"

Hebrews 4:12

Before I conclude this chapter of the book, I want you to understand this, there is nothing we can do that doesn't have some element of risk in it. Everything in life is a risk. Ecclesiastes 10:8 says, "When you work in a quarry, stones might fall and crush you! When you chop wood, there is danger with each stroke of your ax! Such are the risks of life" (NLT).

Eventhough sometimes courageous faith leads to dangerous situations. You can trust that the all-powerful God will continue to equip you and guide you and strengthen you in your battles. No matter what situations or enemies you face, you can be confident because Jesus Christ has won the greatest victory… and that is a great foundation for courageous faith.

Beloved, even if you experience persecution or hardships because of your faith, know that God has the ultimate victory... And He still perform miracles today. In fact, every time you stretch your faith, God does miracles—*every single time*. Today, I encourage you to be bold and daring to live an extraordinary life of courageous faith. I encourage you to release your faith! Because God is shifting things in your favor.

The God that we serve is still in the mountain-moving business. He still moves in the affairs of man, but He only moves when moved by faith. Do not doubt or underestimate what God wants to do in your life. Remember, faith as small as a mustard seed is all you need…If only you can release your faith in uncommon ways, you will see God do uncommon things!

If you make the move, God will make the way.

COURAGEOUS
FAITH

CHAPTER THREE

RELEASING
THE POWER WITHIN!

DID YOU KNOW THERE IS ONE pursuit above all others that this world is after? More than money, more than car or house, more than sex, more than anything... and even more than God. It is the pursuit of the ages — it is the pursuit of **POWER**!

In one form or another, everything this world seeks boils down to the pursuit of power. In Acts 8:9-24, Peter and the other Apostles were experiencing signs, wonders, and miracles after the resurrection of Jesus. A wealthy man named Simon, recognized with worldly power, saw the real power of God flow through the Apostles hands and then offered money to have the Power of God.

Of course, Peter, in his own subtle and soft-spoken way, responded by saying, "May your silver perish with you for thinking that you can obtain the gift of God with money!" (see Acts 8:20) So we see here that the Power of God is far more valuable than money.

In fact, people often use money to obtain power. But the power (*dunamis*) I'm talking about here however, is priceless! And it is the priceless treasure within us. The Power of God that heals is tangible and always available. The woman with the issue of blood tapped it and was healed.

I believe that, as children of God, we all have a Supernatural power with-in us to achieve whatever we want. The only problem is that most of us do not know how to release that power to achieve our heart's desire. God's Word says that there is "power that works in us". It is a tremendous power that shakes the heavens and the earth because it comes from the throne of God, "who is able to do exceedingly abundantly above all that we ask or think"! (see Ephesians 3:30)

God wants us to release that power because there are things that will not happen on earth until we do so. Remember what Jesus said in Matthew 16:19, "...what you bind on earth will be bound in heaven, and whatever you loose on earth will be loosed in heaven." In other words, what you permit to happen, heaven will permit. What you disallow, heaven will disallow!

Friend, the God we serve is a limitless God who is all-powerful, all-knowing, and all-capable. He is the Creator and sustainer of all things. He has matchless power. As those who trust Him and are connected to Him through what Jesus did on the cross to pay the penalty for our sin, we have the privilege of relating to and walking with Him (*the God of all power*).

In this chapter, we are going to deal with the subject of the power and authority of Jesus that has been given to us and the significance of living in that Supernatural power and authority. But before I start, there is something you need to understand. The question is not "How do I get this power and authority from God?" The question is, "What type of person do I need to be in order for God to trust me with His power?"

As I always say, if you are going to learn how to walk in the Supernatural, then you will need to learn to walk hand in hand with God. The Power of God is given by Him through His Spirit. It is not something we earn or manipulate with a formula. It is something we learn to walk in as we learn to walk with Him.

So how do we then live and walk in this *Supernatural* power and authority? There are so many ways, but in this book, we will see two of them.

• The Holy Spirit

• The Living Word of God

The Holy Spirit

The Holy Spirit is the most valuable asset to Christian living. He is the central figure in any breakthrough in life. He is the One in charge of the affairs of the Kingdom of God on earth today; the Chief Executive of divine program on earth. He is behind every exploit in the Kingdom of God. He is also known as the Holy Ghost or the Spirit of God. He is the third Person of the Trinity. He is equal to God the Father and God the Son, but different in function. He is not only the Comforter, He is also the motivator, energizer and operator of every revealed plan (vision) from God.

God had earlier been pouring the Holy Spirit out in drizzles upon prophets, pastors, priests and kings in the old Testament times, enabling them to function in their offices. For instance, until Saul was anointed king of Israel, he could not ascend the throne. (see Samuel 10:1) Elisha could also not stand in the prophet's office until after Elijah had anointed him. (see 1 Kings 19:16). But God never intended that the gift of the **Holy Spirit** be given to only a few people. That was why He spoke through the prophets that a time would come when His Spirit would be poured out, not in drizzles or sprinkles, but in its fullness, upon all flesh. (see Joel 2:28)

No longer will the Holy Spirit be upon a few but upon all who desire Him.

On the last day of the feast, the great day, Jesus stood up and cried out, "If anyone thirsts, let him come to me and drink. Whoever believes in me, as the Scripture has said, Out of his heart will flow rivers of living water."

(Now this he said about the Spirit, whom those who believed in him were to receive, for as yet the Spirit had not been given, because Jesus was not yet glorified.)

John 7:37-39 (ESV)

So until Jesus was *glorified* not everyone who desired the Holy Spirit could have Him.

Releasing the power within!

Today, Christ's authority and power is promised to every believer. There is a power, an authority that is given to the Holy Spirit-filled believer for using in his or her day-to-day walk with Jesus.

The Scripture says,

"And Jesus came and said to them, "All authority in heaven and on earth has been given to me. Go therefore and make disciples of all nations, baptizing them in the name of the Father and of the Son and of the Holy Spirit,"

Matthew 28:18-19 (ESV)

Jesus also said,

"You will receive power when the Holy Spirit has come upon you, and you will be my witnesses in Jerusalem an in all Judea and Samaria, and to the end of the earth."

Acts 1:8 (ESV)

"Behold, I have given you authority to tread on serpents and scorpions, and over all the power of the enemy, and nothing shall hurt you."

Luke 10:19 (ESV)

Above, Jesus was declaring that through the Holy Spirit living within us there would be a resident power that has the ability for us to overcome every obstacle that would come against us (to stop us from being His true witnesses) and can enable us to go to the furthest parts of the earth.

In these days we need to know the reality of that statement — not in word only, but as a practical, outworking experience. When the Holy Spirit comes into our lives He brings with Him the Power of God to enable us to serve God in "the power of His might" (see Ephesians 6:10). The only limitations will be those that we place on ourselves!

The Holy Spirit is the very presence of God's power actively working in His servants (us). As I said earlier, He enables us to be like Him, to have the same power available to us that Jesus had in Him. The Bible says, "How God anointed Jesus of Nazareth with the Holy Spirit and with power ("*dunamis*"), Who went about doing good and healing all who were oppressed by the devil, for God was with Him." (See Acts 10:34-48) The same Holy Spirit now resides within us and we should also be going about doing good and healing all who are oppressed of the devil.

That Supernatural power accompanies the Holy Spirit Who is the Power of God now living inside of you. This power is to make you true witnesses unto the Lord Jesus Christ; not only in your speaking, but in your whole manner of living.

Friend, you must speak the truth of who you really are; a treasured child of God... filled with His Holy Spirit! Far too often we are not able to convince others because we are not convinced ourselves about what God has already given to us by His Spirit. If you say you are filled, baptized in the Holy Spirit, then the anointing and power of God is in the *Holy Spirit* who is now residing within you.

When you begin to realize and understand that God has already given you this power (resident in the Holy Spirit Who is now resident within you), you will accept that truth and rejoice in His Holy Name that you are indeed *"endued with power from on high"* (see Luke 24:49)

The minor prophet, Micah, lived in days when false prophets and ungodly chaos polluted the land; yet he dared to positively confess: "But truly I am full of power by the Spirit of the Lord, and of justice and might, to declare to Jacob his transgression and to Israel his sin." (see Micah 3:8) That was his testimony: he was filled with power by the Spirit of the Lord! This is a power that is more than physical strength; it is a spiritual power, as Zechariah (another minor prophet) declared: it is "not by might nor by power, but by My Spirit, says the Lord of hosts." (see Zechariah 4:6)

Beloved, God does not want you to be ignorant of the mighty gifts of the Holy Spirit in you. In times past satan has even used theologians to cast doubt on the availability of these gifts, but praise God we are learning to pick them up again and use them.

The Bible says in 1 Corinthians 12:8-10, "To one there is given through the Spirit a message of wisdom, to another a message of knowledge by means of the same Spirit, to another faith by the same Spirit, to another gifts of *healing* by that one Spirit, to another miraculous powers, to another prophecy, to another distinguishing between spirits, to another speaking in different kinds of tongues, and to still another the interpretation of tongues."

Greater is the Spirit of God that resides within you than every adversarial and demonic spirit in the world that would oppose you. Whatever battles you are facing in your life, the Holy Spirit will grant you the wisdom and the strength to win them. With Him, you've got power to make impact!

It is my prayer that you embrace the power that lives inside of you (which is the gift of the Holy Spirit), so you can become unstoppable. May the Lord help you to believe that the same Holy Spirit that raised Jesus from the dead, lives inside of you right now! May the God of hope fill you with all joy and peace as you trust in Him overflowing with hope by the power of the Holy Spirit in Jesus Mighty name. Amen!

The Living Word of God

Do you know that the Word of God is a powerful weapon? Apostle Paul referred to it as *"The sword of the Spirit."* He said in Ephesians 6:17, "Take the helmet of salvation and the sword of the Spirit, which is the word of God." The helmet is a very important part of the armor of God in Ephesians 6. The helmet of salvation covers our mind from any attacks of the enemy... It covers us and protects us from any anxiety and negative thoughts injected by the enemy.

After we put on all the defensive items of the armor of God, we can receive the sword of the Spirit, which is the word of God. Among all the items of the armor of God, only the sword of the Spirit (which is the Word of God) is the **defensive** and **offensive** weapon. It is incredibly powerful and effective at driving away the enemy and tearing down his work. It is living and active, sharper than any double-edged sword, and penetrates even to dividing soul and spirit, joints and marrow; it judges the thoughts and attitudes of the heart. (see Hebrews 4:12)

When the constant Word in the Bible (the "logos") becomes the present, instant, and living speaking of the Spirit (the "rhema") to us, this Word is the sword that cuts the enemy into pieces. Friend, words have power when they are God's Words spoken in faith through your lips. The Word of God, spoken in faith in the name of Jesus, has awesome power to overcome seemingly insurmountable obstacles.

This is what the Lord says,

*"For as the rain and snow come down from heaven,
And do not return there without watering the earth,
Making it bear and sprout, And providing seed to the
sower and bread to the eater, So will My word be which
goes out of My mouth; It will not return to Me void
(useless, without result), Without accomplishing what
I desire, And without succeeding in the matter
for which I sent it."*

Isaiah 55:10-11 (AMP)

There is irresistible Supernatural power in God's Word; it will not return to Him empty. God's Word will accomplish His desires and purposes. The King James Version descriptively says that the Word of God will not return void to Him. In other words, it will get the job done! The Living Word of God is the most powerful among all words, because it is guaranteed by God to be effective. When you speak the Word of God, you are tapping into limitless power!

> *"Let the one who has my word speak it faithfully ...*
> *"Is not my word like fire," declares the LORD,*
> *"and like a hammer that breaks a rock in pieces?"*

Jeremiah 23:28-29

Think of the Word of God as a hammer. Picture it. This hammer can drive home a nail = positive results. This hammer can break down obstacles = overcoming negatives. If only you can speak God's Word faithfully, then all kinds of positive things will begin to happen... all kinds of obstacles and opposition will begin to be broken.

Now tell me, what are you speaking over yourself today? Words of LIFE or words of death? Are you speaking God's Word into existence? If you want to start seeing the power of God manifest in your life, you will have to start paying attention to what you say. Jesus certainly understood the power of words, and He used them to change the natural things around Him. When He was tempted by satan in the wilderness, He overcame the devil using one weapon—The Word of God. (see Luke 4:1-13)

Right after He was baptized, Jesus was taken up into a mountain by the Holy Spirit. Forty days had now passed and Jesus fasted the whole time. Now I would say that at this point in His life that Jesus was at His weakest He ever had been—in the natural. But in the spirit, He was at His strongest. He had just spent forty days in direct communication with the Father, getting direction through the Holy Spirit. He was ready for anything!

This is when the devil tried to 'take Him out' you might say. satan came at Jesus with words. Strong words! Words that would try to hurt His pride, words that would offend, words that would get Him to react. satan said to Jesus, "If you are the Son of God, tell these stones to become bread." (see Matthew 4:4) In the natural, Jesus was hungry, but He responded to the devil not through His emotions, but through His spirit. He spoke the Living Word of God over the situation. Jesus said, "It is written: *Man does not live on bread alone, but on every Word that comes out from the mouth of God.*" Three times Jesus spoke to satan: "It is WRITTEN!", and satan's schemes were defeated.

There is great power in the Living Word of God. Thankfully, we don't have to guess what God's Words are. Jesus didn't guess. He quoted the Scriptures (so should we), because the Bible is the Word of God. Don't just "read the Bible", and don't just "read some verses again and again"… exercise your spirit, touch the Lord, and let Him speak to you instantly, presently, and livingly! This becomes your sword to kill the enemy, and you will overcome him by the word of your testimony ! (see Revelation 12:11)

I believe that all of us can be victorious in everything we do when we follow the lead of Jesus. Now I'm not talking about wearing a bracelet that has WWJD (*What Would Jesus Do*) on it. I'm actually talking about speaking the way Jesus did, acting the way Jesus did and actually living His life by every Word of God in whatever situation He found Himself. Today, you may be going through a difficult time in your life. The devil may be using every weapon he has and throwing it right at you. You may be feeling worn down and physically and emotionally weak. But you don't have to stay that way. God's grace is sufficient for you. His strength is perfected in your weakness.

God's Word works against any situation that comes our way every time! Indeed, God's Word is living and active. Once we grab hold of His Word, His Truth, then we can turn any situation around, no matter how destructive it seems to be at the moment. In Jeremiah 1:12, the Lord said, He watches over His Word to perform it. That means that He is waiting to hear you and me speak forth His Words to Him so He can then act on what He said He would do. Once we speak His Word... it is activated and it will come to pass in our lives.

The Living Word of God have life, and it brings life... Jesus said, "The words that I speak unto you, they are spirit, and they are life" (see John 6:63). The Word of God is the anchor our soul should cling to; if you don't feel right within your soul, nothing feels right. And it is only His Word that gives you life, brings you fulfilment and true peace! For they are life to those who find them, and health to all their flesh. (see Proverbs 4:20-22)

We serve a God that *specializes* in our impossibilities. It is only the Living Word of God that can make the world's impossibilities a reality in your life. Your situation might seem hopeless, beyond repair, and even impossible just like the woman with the issue of blood... your dreams, your marriage, your children, are seemingly dead? Friend, God can still interject a BUT! Because He is the One Who can revitalize dead situations! He is the only One who can turn hopeless situations around!

Do you remember Jesus spoken words to dead Lazarus? (see John 11) There is power in the spoken and the written Word of God! Today, learn to declare according to the Word of God...even when you don't feel like it. You have received the power and authority to put the enemy in his place. God has ordained your mouth for victory. So speak Life! Speak life over your family, over your friends, over your marriage, over your business, over your Church, your community, and your nation!

Speak out God's Word to your "Lazarus":

Declare to that addictive behavior *"You have no more control over me, because Jesus has set me free."*

Tell the devil *"Come out, because you are overcome by the blood of the Lamb."*

Command that cancer *"Leave this body, because by the wounds of Jesus I am healed."*

Speak to your Finances *"come into line, because my God shall supply all my needs according to His riches in glory."*

Command Drugs/alcohol *"I don't need you, because the Son of God has set me free!"*

An uncontrollable habit? Declare *"I am more than a conqueror through Him (CHRIST) that loved me!"*

Beloved, whatever situation you find yourself in, you must know that you are not at a standstill, you are not at a dead end. Your godly weapons are mighty to the pulling down of *strongholds.* (see 1 Corinthians 10:4) All I want you to understand is that if you are under the authority of God, you have the power of God through Jesus Christ and the Holy Spirit. Once you realize this, you have already won against the attacks of the enemy. The power and authority has been given but you need to make it active… and you do that only through meditating God's Word by the help of the Holy Spirit. Also through prayer, fasting and worship.

Trust me, nothing the devil can throw against you will be able to take you down or out…if you respond with the Word of God in faith. I decree and declare that from today, you will operate with power and authority of God through Christ Jesus… to open any door you have faith to walk through… and it will be open for you in Jesus name. Amen!

If you make the move, God will make the way.

COURAGEOUS
FAITH

CHAPTER FOUR

THE MASTER'S TOUCH

IT WAS 1818 IN FRANCE, AND LOUIS, a boy of 9, was sitting in his father's workshop. The father was a harness-maker and the boy loved to watch his father work the leather. "Someday father," said Louis, "I want to be a harness-maker, just like you." "Why not start now?" said the father.

He took a piece of leather and drew a design on it. "Now, my son," he said, "take the hole-puncher and a hammer and follow this design, but be careful that you don't hit your hand." excited, the boy began to work, but when he hit the hole-puncher, it flew out of his hand and pierced his eye! He lost the sight of that eye immediately. Later, sight in the other eye failed. Louis was now totally blind.

A few years later, Louis was sitting in the family garden when a friend handed him a pinecone. As he ran his sensitive fingers over the cone, an idea came to him. He became enthusiastic and began to create an alphabet of raised dots on paper so that the blind could feel and interpret what was written. Thus, Louis Braille opened a whole new world to those who are blind through the power of touch.

Humans, at least when things are working as they should, possess 5 senses. These are sight, hearing, taste, smell and touch. All of them are important to our existence in and understanding of the world around us. While they are all important, and I wouldn't want to be without any, the sense of touch is one that places us into direct contact with our world.

When we TOUCH something, we are becoming intimately involved with that thing. While I have heard of people losing some, or all of the other senses, I have never heard of a person losing their sense of touch. Can you imagine not being able to touch your world? Can you imagine not being able to touch those you love? To not to be able to touch them might be worse that to not be able to see them!

We all touch thousands of things every day of our lives. Most, we do not even think about. But, there are times when we reach out and deliberately touch objects because we want to connect with that object. Our touch might be that of love, of passion, of tenderness, of compassion, of help, of deliverance or of curiosity. Our touch could involve many other emotions and processes that I didn't mention. Often, our touch can effect change in the objects we touch.

In this chapter, I want to talk about a touch that is far superior to any other human touch. I want to talk about the touch of Christ, and remind you that His touch is the touch of God! When He extends His hand into your life and purposely touches you, He will produces changes that no other touch can duplicate.

Before, let me ask you this; "Have you ever been in a place of prayer where you needed just a little touch of Jesus?" Jesus Christ is the Master Healer and He has a plan to bring healing to our lives. In fact, our every blessing is found in the person of Jesus. Everyone who encounters Him never leaves the same. He is the only One who can free you from the guilt of your past and the labels that have been put on you.

Just one touch of His Love is more than enough. One encounter with Jesus will change your life forever. Do you remember how Jesus changed the life of the woman with the issue of blood through the power of His touch? We read that this desperate, hopeless, helpless woman decided she would carefully and secretly sneak up through the crowd and ever so barely touch just the hem of Jesus garment. Even though according to the Jewish Law, this "issue of blood" made her unclean... she still had this "crazy" idea; "If only Jesus would touch her, she would be healed." But that could not happen because she would defile Him. So... "If He would not touch her... she would touch Him". Courageous faith in action!

And the Bible says, she thought to herself that if all she did was to touch Jesus, she would get well... She reached out her hand and touched the hem of Jesus cloak. Immediately the flow of her blood was dried up; and she felt in her body that she was healed of her affliction.

Like this woman, we are all looking for the touch of Jesus (*the Master*); reconciliation where there is conflict, restoration where there is *discouragement*, righteousness when we feel the burden of our sin. Reassurance when we feel incapable of what the Lord is calling us for, renewal if we are sick, recovery if we are blind, resurrection if anything is dead in our life. We all need that Supernatural encounter that leaves us speechless and transformed!

Beloved, the Lord's desire is for us to enjoy the blessings, the healing, health and wholeness that He has purchased for us at Calvary. Jesus went to the scourging post and then the cross to pay the full price for our health and wholeness. The same Jesus who healed that woman in Mark 5, and all who came to Him for a miracle when He was on earth is the same Jesus who wants to change your life for the better.

He said,

"The Spirit of the Sovereign LORD is on me, because the LORD has anointed me to proclaim good news to the poor. He has sent me to bind up the brokenhearted, to proclaim freedom for the captives and release from darkness for the prisoners, to proclaim the year of the LORD's favor and the day of vengeance of our God, to comfort all who mourn, and provide for those who grieve in Zion – to bestow on them a crown of beauty instead of ashes, the oil of joy instead of mourning, and a garment of praise instead of a spirit of despair. They will be called oaks of righteousness, a planting of the LORD for the display of his splendor."

Isaiah 61:1-3

This is why Jesus came! He came to give us Life! He came that we may have life and that we might have it more abundantly. (see John 10:10) He wants the broken hearts to be bound up, the captives and prisoners to be proclaimed free, and a crown of beauty to emerge from ashes. Instead of mourning, He brings the oil of joy. Instead of a spirit of despair, He clothes us with a garment of praise! The Master healer came to bring us into healing, deliverance and wholeness.

Friend, everything you can ever want is in Jesus. If you want to do exploits… heal the sick, cast out devils, impact your generation, overcoming the storms of life, possess your promised land, experience Supernatural healing, restoration, financial breakthrough, or the favor of God in every aspect… then all you need is a touch from the Master!

Jesus Christ is the only way to a victorious life! If you will believe and trust in Him today, He will fulfill His Word to you. The Bible reassures us that Jesus is the same yesterday, today and forever. If you are sick, He will heal you, oppressed, He will deliver you, if you are barren, He will give you fruitfulness. Clearly, the One whom God has chosen to rule the earth is a warm, compassionate Person who not only cares for people but also has the power to help them!

As I said in my book (*The Lord Is My Shepherd*), Jesus is our good Shepherd. He has what we need! He even wants to give it to us. Let's reach for it and see what happens!... Miracles, Signs, and Wonders!

The Divine Encounter

True change requires a significant encounter with God. When an ordinary man meets the extraordinary God, his life is never the same again. It takes an encounter with God to become a man and a woman of impact. It takes an encounter with God to counter the agenda of the enemy!

Encountering God is necessary to our spiritual life and our spirit man. Once we have a divine encounter with the God of the Supernatural, we can operate in the Supernatural. The truth is that, every encounter with God delivers specific package. Every encounter with the Word of God is an encounter with power.

What, therefore, is the power of Divine encounter? Divine encounter sets you on the path of destiny fulfillment. One can never be the same after having an encounter with God. Having an encounter with Him will cause somethings to shift in you, around you and for you. When God (the Father, Son or the Holy Spirit) touches an individual, it brings about instant healing or miracle, it releases Supernatural strength.

An encounter with Jesus is what makes one to count in life. The woman with the issue of blood, for instance became a notable person in her generation as a result of a Divine encounter. When you encounter Jesus, He changes your life to reflect who you are in Him. He changes you from an outcast to a child of God because you are adopted into the family of God. He changes your character from a state of *unrighteousness* to a state of righteousness in the eyes of God. He changes your position from the rejected of God to the Elect of God. And He changes you from being separated from God to being sealed by the Holy Ghost.

Every encounter with Jesus brings an end to every storm in our lives and brings peace that surpasses all understanding. An encounter with Jesus guarantees total transformation of life and destiny. Once you have a divine encounter with Jesus, your life will become a living testimony…you will not need to be told that you have been touched by God, but you will just know. Because a *divine encounter* comes with deep revelations of secrets hidden and breaking of curses. Everything that is in your life that does not belong there must go! There are things that were lurched onto you that will begin to fall off. Poverty will fall off, sickness will disappear, and curses will be broken.

Now my question is, "Do you want to experience God from the natural to the Supernatural? Are you ready to have an encounter with God today and let your Life forever experience a new change in Jesus Name?! If yes, then keep on reading! ☺

We all need an encounter with the true and living God. Nothing less is sufficient. You need an encounter with Jesus to start a relationship with God the Father. God, the Creator, wants to be in a relationship with us, His creation. That is why He made us in the first place. And it is the only way we will be truly fulfilled in life. The Scripture says; In God's presence is fullness of joy; At His right Hand are pleasures forever. Draw near to

God and He will draw near to you. The Bible also declare in the Book of Psalms, "The LORD is near to all who call upon Him, to all who call upon Him in truth." (see Psalm 145:18)

Our God has not left us. Through the sacrifice of Jesus, we have been filled with the very Spirit of God (The Holy Spirit) who longs to reveal to us daily the nearness and love of our heavenly Father. We are never alone. There is nowhere we can flee from the presence of our God. He said, "My Presence will go with you, and I will give you rest." (see Exodus 33:14)

Believe it or not, God is closer than you think. He is reaching for you. And He is going to break down every barrier and reach through every wall until He touches you. But in order for it to happen you must believe in it first. You have to desire it with all your heart and with a strong faith just like the woman with the issue of blood... Go to Jesus in humility. Tell Him specifically what you need...through prayer and supplication with thanksgiving. Feel His Divine touch. Believe you are forgiven. And know you are loved!

Beloved, life is not just ordinary but also has a Supernatural side. It is that element that is needed in your life to make all the difference and determine the course of life. You need to encounter Heaven and experience the reality of Jesus. You may have been raised with the belief that, Jesus is a myth and a story of man, or that He has nothing to do with your life, my friend, I have good news for you, Jesus is alive and real. And He wants to do a miracle in your life today!

The divine touch of God saves the sinner, heals the sick, and delivers the oppressed. The divine encounter sanctifies the believer, strengthens the weak, and restores those who have gone astray. It is the divine touch of God that empowers us... and recreates us to be conformed to the image of the Son of God—Jesus.

As I mentioned earlier, until God touches you, you cannot have an experience with the Supernatural. It's a divine encounter that makes all the difference. Paul who was Saul got to know Jesus in a fresh way, and it changed the course of his destiny and life. Trust me, you cannot meet heaven and be the same again. I totally agree with Pastor Enoch Adeboye when he said, "Every Man born of a woman needs the divine touch of God" Being born again is okay; being filled with the Holy Ghost is also okay; but if you want to walk in a world of miracles, a world of the impossible... you need the divine touch of God upon your life. You need the Supernatural touch of the Master!

God absolutely loves the humble. He comes to those who are seeking Him. The Saints throughout the Bible were humble in their seeking after God. They were righteous in their character and prayed earnestly with reverence to Him. God consistently met them where they were and encountered them. He launched them into extraordinary lives. The same is true today! God still moves in this way.

I don't know the kind of touch you need in your life today, but I know Who can give it to you! Jesus is His name and touching lives is His fame. Whether you are lost, backslidden, burdened, discouraged, or just want to learn to love Him more, you need His touch. Know this: God has great plans for you in Jesus Christ! Come to Christ today! He alone can restore beauty to a ruined life. He alone can satisfy and save your thirsty soul.

Say this prayer with me…

"Lord Jesus, for too long I've kept You out of my life. I know that I am a sinner and that I cannot save myself. No longer will I close the door when I hear You knocking. By faith I gratefully receive Your gift of salvation. I am ready to trust You as my Lord and Savior. Thank You, Lord Jesus, for coming to earth. I believe You are the Son of God who died on the cross for my sins and rose from the dead on the third day. Thank You for bearing my sins and giving me the gift of Eternal life. I believe Your Words are true. Come into my heart, Lord Jesus, and be my Savior. Amen!"

If you make the move, God will make the way.

COURAGEOUS
FAITH

CHAPTER FIVE

THE WAITING

THERE ARE TOUGH TIMES IN LIFE when you just question if God is out there. Believing that God can take you safely through the storms of this life can be difficult. As I said in one of my books (*PUSH*)... God's timing doesn't always line up with our way of doing things and it may seem that we are alone in our battles.

There are periods of our lives in which it is easy to believe. There are also periods in which questions come. We don't go looking for the doubts, but they come looking for us. We join a long line of people who have been asked to believe something that seems impossible from our perspective. This is especially true when your dream becomes a nightmare and you find yourself in the starring role.

In life, every person must face the difficulty that comes when God's timing does not line up with our own; what is the desperate job seeker to do when the employment doesn't come through? How does the married couple face another childless year when everyone around them has caught the pregnancy bug? How much longer does the single woman have to wait for a good man? Will science ever find a cure for the illness plaguing the young person in chronic pain?

Our response to these sometimes gnawing questions is a matter of faith: Do you really believe that God loves you; that He has given you every spiritual blessing; that even in the midst of heartache He is working for the good; that He is truly trustworthy? — Often when our prayers are not answered and our faith waivers we have a choice to make. We can stay stuck in doubt or we can choose to trust God's timing and believe what the Bible says about His plans for our lives.

In this last chapter, I want us to talk about the other principal character in the story of Mark 5:21-42... Jairus! The Bible tells us that he was one of the rulers of the Synagogue. That means Jairus was a man of great power and prestige. He was a man who had it all together... that is, until his beloved daughter became gravely ill. The Scripture says,

"When Jesus had again crossed over by boat to the other side of the lake, a large crowd gathered around him while he was by the lake. Then one of the synagogue leaders, named Jairus, came, and when he saw Jesus, he fell at his feet. He pleaded earnestly with him, "My little daughter is dying. Please come and put your hands on her so that she will be healed and live." So Jesus went with him.

Mark 5:21-24

So when Jairus, a man of power, position and prestige, saw his daughter grow sicker by the day, he was alarmed because there was nothing he could do. But he knew that Jesus was around. I don't know whether Jairus was a believer in Jesus at this point. But he knew that Jesus was the one who could touch his daughter. Maybe he had a basic faith that he was beginning to exercise. So he found Jesus, and they went on their way to Jairus house to see his sick little girl (she was twelve years old).

I think Jairus must have been filled with hope, thinking, everything is going to be all right; *"I have Jesus here. He will do something special."* But suddenly our courageous woman arrived on the scene (☺…you know who I'm talking about right? The woman with the issue of blood.) As we read earlier, she came out of nowhere and caused a big scene. She touched the hem of Jesus garment and was instantly healed. Jesus stopped to talk to her. They had a whole conversation right there. The Scriptures says, while Jairus waited on Jesus, a servant from his house found him and said, *"Your daughter is dead; Why trouble the Teacher any further?"* (see Mark 5:35) In other words, your daughter is dead boss... there is no need that Jesus come. He cannot help you now.

Here Jairus was in dire need of a miracle, and he was so close to getting that blessing. And, not only does someone sneak in and steal Jesus time, but his window of opportunity closed. I bet you can identify with Jairus. We have all waited on God and have seen others step ahead of us in line. It can feel like our blessing completely passed us by while God was busy doing something else.

I know I have felt like Jairus before. Years ago, when I wanted to lunch my ministry officially, I didn't understand why God wanted me to wait and help others to finish their projects while I thought I was ready. But, a year later, I realized the Lord had saved me from *beginning* my ministry internationally without a solid foundation and a good plan.

I am not going to deny that waiting on God is hard. But an important lesson that I am continuing to learn each day is that God works things out in His own perfect timing. Trusting in God and His timing, I believe is the key to success and happiness in life.

In my book (*God Is Up To Something Great*) I wrote about how God's delays are not necessarily God's denials. In our waiting God is working. The truth is that God never forgets… and even when it looks like nothing is happening, He continues to orchestrate things in the background so that at the right time, the outcome will be abundantly above what we could have imagined!

Beloved, waiting on God is never wasting time. Perhaps we misunderstand what waiting is all about. The Free dictionary defines waiting as "The act of remaining inactive or stationary." But for us believes, waiting is not passive. It is an activity. It is quiet, active stillness. It is a directed, purposeful expectancy.

Waiting on God is a *definite* directing of our attention toward Him… waiting for His intervention in our circumstances and waiting for further instructions.

We are all waiting on God at different times in our lives. For you, it could be that baby you have been longing to hold in your arms, an illness to be healed, a family member or friend to come to the Lord, a break-through in your marriage or finances, to start a business, a door to be opened, whatever it is we are left waiting. You have probably heard the old saying "good things come to those who wait."

Sometimes it is hard to understand why God doesn't allow things to happen straightaway. All the while people keep telling you to trust in God and the right thing will come along and to be honest they start to sound like just words. Platitudes with not much meaning. They lose their impact and you start to lose a bit of hope; what if God isn't going to answer my prayer? Time is running out. How do I keep trusting when it seems like nothing is changing?

I don't know what Jairus thought, but I can just imagine that he may have been thinking, "*This woman, sick as she may be, would have lived another day. Why is Jesus stopping to speak to her now?*" It's curious... how easy it is to dismiss the need of others as insignificant when we compare them to our own. So often we can't see beyond our own needs. And that is why Jesus dealings were so often surprising... even disturbing to everyone.

It was the tax collectors, notorious sinners, lepers, and immoral women who reached His heart. He had as much concern for the nameless, insignificant, poor, and chronically sick woman as He had for this obviously "deserving" ruler of the synagogue.

Listen, people matter to Jesus! All kinds of people, not just the rich, influential, "good" folks. This woman was "unclean," destitute, and isolated, but despite how others looked at her, Jesus wouldn't risk losing her in the crowd. His compassion extended beyond a mere healing; He wanted to make sure she was set free from bondage and at peace with God.

Jesus said to her,

> *"Daughter, your faith has healed you.*
> *Go in peace and be freed from your suffering."*

Mark 5:34

God's timetable may move slowly, but it does move surely. In an emergency room, if a doctor treats a patient with a nosebleed while another patient with a heart attack goes unattended and dies, that doctor is in trouble. If a police officer chases someone for speeding but ignores a bank robbery, that officer could face discipline. Some situations call for immediate attention, while others can wait. Yet in our story Jesus seems to delay an urgent case to deal with a less-important one.

Even though Jesus stopped to bless another, He didn't forget about Jairus. Jesus heard what the servant had to say and told Jairus in Mark 5:36, "**Don't be afraid; just believe.**" Luck 8:50 put it this way, "*Fear not: believe only, and she shall be made whole.*" I like to think that if this were occurring in our modern day, Jesus would have said, "Don't panic." That is our first reaction after all… When we think that we have missed our chance, we freak out, go into mourning or sulk into bitterness. But that is not always necessary.

The Lord says,

> *"Do not fear, for I am with you. Do not be afraid, for I am your God. I will give you strength, and for sure I will help you. Yes, I will hold you up with My right hand that is right and good."*

Isaiah 41:10 (NLV)

Maybe you have waited for Jesus to help you, but it seemed never to happen. Friend, I have a good news for you! The Lord said I should tell you, "Don't be afraid. Hold on to your faith, and you will have what you ask for."

Remember: Jesus is never late. He is always on time—but it's always in His time, and His timing is best. I don't know what you are facing today, but I encourage you to wait patiently and trust the process. God has a plan. He is a good God and He is so faithful and true to His promises. If the answer to your prayer seems slow in coming, wait patiently, for it will surely take place. It will not be delayed. (see Habakkuk 2:3)

One thing I have learned in my journey with the Lord is that, He never leaves us and He always provides… even when we don't see a way through it. God doesn't work on our time but He is always on time. Indeed, God is worth waiting for; His time is always best!

Talitha koum!

We know that wherever Jesus is present... there is outpouring of grace leading to repentance, salvation and victorious life. As I always say, " Wherever Jesus is...there is resurrection...there is Life!"

The Bible tells us that eventually Jesus made His way to Jairus house with three of His disciples; Peter, James and John. In the midst of the wailers and mourners, He said rather calmly, "Why all this commotion and wailing? The child is not dead but asleep." But they laughed at Him. Then the Bible says, He made them all go outside, and took the child's father and mother and the disciples who were with Him, and went in where the child was. He took her by the hand and said to her, "Talitha koum!" Immediately the girl stood up and began to walk around. At this they were completely astonished.

What does "TALITHA KOUM" mean? **Talitha** is an Aramaic word, a diminutive, and literally, it means 'little girl'... but culturally, it would have been the way that a parent would refer to their own child. **Koum** doesn't mean 'rise from the dead', it means 'get up', as in 'awaken'! So *"Talitha koum"* simply means "Little girl, I say to you, get up!" (see Mark 5:41) I love Pastor Timothy J. Keller's paraphrase: "Honey, it's time to get up!"

Literally, Jesus took the little girl's hand and said, "Honey, it's time to get up!" and she opened her eyes and raised up and walked. And the Bible says, they were greatly astonished. But I think astonished is an understatement, don't you think? Jairus wanted to bring Jesus to his house so He could cure a fever (heal his daughter), not perform a resurrection!

The amazing thing is that when you go to Jesus for help, you get from Him far more than you had in mind! But remember, you also end up giving Him far more that you expected to. Jairus had a plan; go find Jesus, talk Him into coming home with him, and hopefully get Him there before his little girl died. But after his daughter died (*due to the delay of the Great Physician*), The Master Healer — Jesus looks him right in the eye and says, "*Don't be afraid! Just trust me!*" Under those circumstances, that is asking a lot, isn't it?

Now, of course, when we read the story to the end, we know something that Jairus and the disciples didn't know: we know that to Jesus, curing a fever, or raising someone from the dead was no different. Jesus has power over death. He can take a *superstitious* woman who has a healing and turn her into a life long disciple. The people with Jesus in that moment had no clue about either ability. No idea at all!

It seemed to Jairus and the disciples that Jesus was delaying for no good reason, but they didn't have all the facts. And so often, if our God and heavenly Father seems to be unconscionably delaying His grace in our life, it's because there is some crucial information that we don't yet have, some essential variable that Is unavailable to us. As the matter of fact, in God there is nothing as delay. What we call "delay", to Him, it is called divine alignment.

You see, some things can never be rushed. An excellent example is the birth of a baby. There will always be a waiting period of approximately nine months from the time a child is conceived to when he or she is born. Some things actually turn out better when we wait for them. The skin of a banana has a green color when it is plucked off a tree. But the banana will taste better if you wait until the skin turns yellow before eating it. Other items like cheese taste better when they are "aged."

During seasons of waiting God continues to work in us. While waiting might seem a waste of time, God designed it to be productive. The exercise of waiting is shaping and sharpening. Through it the Lord instills humility, patience and peace in our hearts and minds. When it looks as though the Lord is not listening to us and has put an obstacle in our path. What we need to understand is that... He wants us to rise to the occasion. He wants us to exercise our faith. He wants us to step forward and not give up so easily.

Yet, sadly, so many times when we ask God to do something, and He doesn't do it. We throw in the towel...we say, *"Forget it!"* Dear friend, be persistent! The woman with the issue of blood was. And Jairus, if he was being tested, certainly came through this with flying colors. He realized that this was not an interruption, but an opportunity. He not only accepted Jesus, but also His timing.

This is where a lot of people have trouble with God. But as I have said many times, there are three ways that God answers prayer: "*Yes, no and wait.*" I hate the answer wait. Who wants to wait? But here is what we need to be careful of. Don't try to take matters into your own hands, because you can make a bigger mess of it. Jesus does not ask for our understanding of His ways and timing; He asks for our trust. He got this from the desperately ill woman and from Jairus. What about you?

It's been said that we do not know what the future holds, but we believe in a God who holds our future. Beloved, worrying about the future robs you of the present. Worrying would not change your situation so enjoy your life and appreciate God's goodness in your life. Today, count your blessings, name them one by one.

You are never an afterthought to Jesus — the Prince of Peace. He knows all, sees all, and is touched with the things that trouble you. He knows your suffering and how it hurts sometimes to wait. However, He is on His way to your house to take the remains of your dream and resurrect it. Don't be afraid, just believe!

All who believe will hear their own
"Talitha koum!"

CONCLUSION

CHOOSE FAITH OVER FEAR

A WISE MAN ONCE SAID, "Life without faith is a life with fear!" If one has no faith in God he is left to live by his own power and strength. While this might carry someone for a while, in the end it is not enough!

Choosing faith over fear is a choice every believer can't avoid — either we are walking in faith or fear. God demands that we walk by faith. It isn't optional. "For God has not given us a spirit of fear, but of power and of love and of a sound mind." (see 2 Timothy 1:7) His desire is that we walk with Him one step at a time. The truth is that, the enemy is the author of fear, not God. God is Love...Love drives away fear and fear cannot reign where Love exist! In other words, fear and faith cannot coexist; where you have one, you cannot have the other. You need to choose!

Did you know that fear works just like faith but in the opposite direction? Faith opens the door for God to work in our lives; fear opens the door for the enemy to work in our lives. The truth of the matter is, fear and faith are both expectations; faith expects the best and fear expects the worst.

Now my last question for you in this book is; "What are you expecting? Are you expecting the very best or are you expecting the worst?"

Beloved, fear is a choice. And so is faith. Like Pastor Rick Warren said, "When we choose fear over faith, it makes us skeptical...we are afraid of trying anything new when we are afraid. It makes us selfish...we are afraid to commit to God and to others. It makes us shortsighted...we focus on the past and not on the future."

Fear always tells you what you are not, what you don't have, what you can't do, and what you never will be. It is a tactic that the devil uses to hinder your faith and keep you from accomplishing God's will for your life, but you don't have to give in. Remember that Jesus overcame that fear; He left it no power and no strength. It has **NO-thing** over you!

No matter what you are facing in your life, you have to make a choice to be confident and to feel secure; God is on your side! The Bible says, "Who the Son set free is free indeed." (see John 8:36) You are delivered from fear through Christ Jesus! God has given you authority and freedom to choose. So today choose to exhibit faith and boldness and start enjoying the liberating freedom from fear.

Perhaps you feel like you are surrounded by difficulties in this particular season of your life. Maybe the enemy's armies (satan and his demons) seem to have an overwhelming advantage over you. Don't you worry! "For the Lord your God is going with you! He will fight for you against your enemies, and He will give you victory!" (see Deuteronomy 20:4 NLT)

Before you close this book, I encourage you to make the right choice today just like Jairus and the woman with the blood issue. When fear knocks on the door, answer with faith! Don't let fear keep you from moving forward in the plan of God for your life. I firmly believe that you are entering a new season in your life! Be open to walk by faith into this new level of Abundance in the Kingdom! Don't be blinded by your natural circumstances. Instead, ask God to increase your faith and open your spiritual eyes to see beyond your circumstances. Make up your mind that you will not bow down to fear. You have already made the decision that you will not be afraid.

Like Paul, "I pray that the eyes of your heart may be enlightened, so that you will know what is the hope of His (God) calling... and what is the surpassing greatness of His power toward us who believe." (see Ephesians 1: 18-19) Friend, God has brought you through before and He will bring you through again. Make a decision, each day to choose faith over fear. And remember, God always has your best interest in mind. According to the Psalmist, loads of benefits are the allocation of every child of God.

"Blessed be the Lord, Who daily loads us with benefits,
The God of our salvation!"

Psalm 68:19 (NKJV)

Faith is our covenant access for all the glorious benefit in the Kingdom. Your belief in the ability of God will cause a release of your daily allocation of benefits. (see James 1:5-7) Our faith in God and His Word is what pleases the heart of God, so don't sit back in doubt or fear... ask what you know is in His Word for you, and confidently expect to see it become your reality!

Courageous Faith can provoke a turn around at any time. So get ready! And always remember, every story is re-writable by faith. Every Red sea is crossable by faith...and every wall of Jericho is collapsible by faith.

Courageous Faith has the spiritual capacity to re-package every man's destiny. Choose faith today so you can overcome fear and live in the freedom and victory God has in store for you!

As you choose faith over fear,
may God back you up in Jesus Mighty name!

AMEN!

ABOUT THE AUTHOR

Determined, Innovative, Anointed, and Cutting Edge are some words often used to describe JERRY BONSU. Founder and Senior minister of Victory Life International Center (VLIC), a revolutionary Movement of 'like minded' and 'like spirited' people coming together in one accord: whose mission is to empower and equip individuals through teaching and preaching the uncompromised Word of God, and helping them to fulfill their highest calling and usher them into a supernatural lifestyle of faith and abundant living.

Jerry Bonsu is a visionary leader who merges multimedia, the marketplace, and faith into one dynamic calling. He is also the visionary and founder behind several entities, including: Victory in Praise International Gathering, a vibrant, dynamic worship conference, which brings together more than 2000 people each gathering, —a wide audience of pastors, worship leaders, artists, musicians, scholars, students, and other interested worshipers. Founder and President of Jerry Bonsu Ministries (JBM); Jerry is also the leader of a gospel group Jerry Bonsu & Levitical Anointing; And the co-founder of a non-profit organization Elyon Foundation, created to influence the next generation.

Jerry Bonsu —dynamic conference speaker, author, life coach, entrepreneur, worship leader... also travels throughout the world with his breakthrough teaching on understanding your God-given identity, purpose, and destiny in Christ. His mission is to impact his generation with divine revelation. Jerry and his wife, Laetitia are the proud parents of two children, Janelle Kierra and Janessa Kimani.

Connect With Jerry!

Website: JerryBonsu.org
Speaking engagements: bookjerry@jerrybonsu.org
Facebook: Facebook.com/jerrybonsuministries
Instagram: Instagram.com/jerrybonsu
Twitter: Twitter.com/jerrybonsu
Youtube: Youtube.com/jerrybonsu
PUSH Conference: Jerrybonsu.org/Push
To join the mailing list: JerryBonsu.org

BOOKS & CD'S BY JERRY BONSU

* PUSH

* The Path to Victory

* Dear Dreamer

* God Is Up To Something Great

* Step Into Your Purpose

* The Power Of I AM

* The Power Of I AM (Audio Book)

* I AM Who God Says I AM

* The Lord Is My Shepherd

* Victory Noise (Album)

Grow deeper in your Christian Faith with a wide selection of CD'S & books written by **JERRY BONSU**
Visit jerrybonsu.org

Order these inspiring products and more by visiting
www.jerrybonsu.org and be sure to join us on Facebook, Twitter &
Instagram for more inspirational words.

WWW.JERRYBONSU.ORG

www.ingramcontent.com/pod-product-compliance
Lightning Source LLC
Chambersburg PA
CBHW060656030426
42337CB00017B/2652